HOW DID THAT GET TO MY TABLE?

ICE CREAM

BY PAM ROSENBERG

COMMUNITY CONNECTIONS ?

CHERRY LAKE
Publishing

Published in the United States of America by Cherry Lake Publishing
Ann Arbor, Michigan
www.cherrylakepublishing.com

Content Advisers: Anuradha Prakash, PhD, Professor of Food Science, Chapman University
Reading Adviser: Cecilia Minden-Cupp, PhD, Literacy Consultant

Photo Credits: Cover and page 1, ©Sters, used under license from Shutterstock, Inc.; page 5,
©Samuel Acosta, used under license from Shutterstock, Inc.; page 7, ©2windspa/
Dreamstime.com; page 9, ©Donald Gargano, used under license from Shutterstock, Inc.;
page 11, ©MichaelTaylor, used under license from Shutterstock, Inc.; page 13, ©Nigel Cattlin/
Alamy; page 15, ©Jeff Greenberg/Alamy; page 17, ©AP Photo/Journal Times, Mark Hertzberg;
page 19, ©Noah Strycker, used under license from Shutterstock, Inc.; page 21, ©Jaimie Duplass,
used under license from Shutterstock, Inc.

LIBRARY OF CONGRESS CATALOGING-IN-PUBLICATION DATA
Rosenberg, Pam.
  How did that get to my table? Ice cream / by Pam Rosenberg.
    p. cm.—(Community connections)
  Includes index.
  ISBN-13: 978-1-60279-467-2
  ISBN-10: 1-60279-467-7
  1. Ice cream, ices, etc. I. Title. II. Title: Ice cream. III. Series.
  TX795.R625 2009
  637'.4—dc22   2008054796

Cherry Lake Publishing would like to acknowledge the
work of The Partnership for 21st Century Skills. Please
visit www.21stcenturyskills.org for more information.

ICE CREAM

CONTENTS

HOW DID THAT GET TO MY TABLE?

CREAMY, COLD, AND YUMMY

You can eat it in a cone. You can eat it in a bowl. Sometimes you top it with hot fudge and whipped cream. It is perfect on a hot day. What is it? Ice cream!

Ice cream comes in many different flavors.

Did you ever wonder how ice cream gets to your table? It all starts on a dairy farm.

Milk is the main **ingredient** in ice cream. Workers milk the cows at the farm. **Tanker trucks** bring the milk to a factory. The trucks are **refrigerated** to keep the milk cold.

Tanker trucks that carry milk must be kept very clean. That helps keep the milk safe to drink.

Look at a carton of ice cream. Do you see the list of ingredients? Which ingredient is listed first? That is the main ingredient. The ice cream contains more of it than any other ingredient.

AT THE ICE CREAM FACTORY

What happens at the factory? The milk is pumped into big storage tanks. Now it is time to make the ice cream. Pipes carry the milk to a **blender**. Sugar, eggs, and other ingredients are added to the blender. Then all of the ingredients are blended together.

Milk and cream are stored in tanks. The tanks keep the milk and cream cold so they don't spoil.

8

MILK

CREAM

CREAM

9

Ice cream is cold when you eat it. But the next step in making ice cream is heating the mixture! The mixture is heated to kill **bacteria**. Bacteria could spoil the ice cream. Then it would taste bad. The bacteria might even make people sick.

Bacteria are so small you can't see them without a microscope. Under a microscope, some of them look like this.

THINK!

Workers in food factories are very careful about bacteria. Can you think of some ways workers could help keep food safe? Hint: what are some things your family does to keep food fresh and your kitchen clean?

11

Next, the heated ice cream mixture is pumped through small holes or a screen. This **homogenizes** the ice cream mix. Homogenizing helps the ingredients stay mixed together. Then the ice cream mixture is cooled. It gets pumped into a big tank. Then it stays in the tank for a few hours. This gives the ingredients more time to blend.

A worker makes sure that the machines that heat ice cream work properly.

Do you like chocolate ice cream? Maybe strawberry is your favorite. Then you will like what happens next. Flavorings are added to the ice cream.

Now the ice cream is frozen. Air is added by stirring the ice cream as it freezes. This keeps the ice cream mix soft, like soft-serve ice cream.

There are many different pipes and machines in an ice cream factory.

ICE CREAM FREEZER

The last step is adding chunky ingredients. This is when pieces of fruit, candy, or nuts are added. Then the ice cream is ready for **packaging**.

Machines fill cartons with ice cream. Machines also put lids on the cartons. Then the cartons go into a very cold freezer or through a very cold tunnel. That's where the ice cream is frozen hard.

A worker checks cartons of ice cream that have just been filled.

FROM FACTORY TO STORE TO TABLE

Ice cream is stored in a **warehouse**. Then it is shipped to stores. Can you guess what kind of truck takes ice cream to stores? If you said a freezer truck, you're correct!

At the store, the ice cream is put in freezer cases. That's where you can find your favorite flavor.

Look for ice cream in the frozen food section of your grocery store.

ASK QUESTIONS!

Do you know someone who drives a delivery truck? Ask him or her about that job. What is it like to drive a truck? Asking questions is a good way to learn about different jobs.

19

Scoop some ice cream into a bowl. Your tasty treat has traveled far.

Now it is time for the last stop. Pick up your spoon and dig in!

Now you know how ice cream gets to your table.

GLOSSARY

bacteria (bak-TIHR-ee-uh) very small living things that can spoil food or make people sick

blender (BLEN-dur) a machine that mixes food

homogenizes (huh-MOJ-uh-nize-ez) makes small bits of something all the same size so they stay mixed together

ingredient (in-GREE-dee-uhnt) one of the items that a product is made from

packaging (PAK-ij-ing) putting a product in its container or wrapping

refrigerated (ri-FRIJ-uh-ray-ted) kept cold

tanker trucks (TANG-kur TRUKS) trucks that have large tanks for carrying liquids

warehouse (WAIR-hous) a large building used for storing food or other products

FIND OUT MORE

BOOKS

Gibbons, Gail. *Ice Cream: The Full Scoop*. New York: Holiday House, 2006.

Keller, Kristin Thoennes. *From Milk to Ice Cream*. Mankato, MN: Capstone Press, 2005.

WEB SITES

Dr. Spock—Thirteen Fun Facts about Ice Cream
www.drspock.com/article/0,1510,5941,00.html
Learn some interesting and unusual facts about ice cream

MakeIceCream.com—Coffee Can Ice Cream
www.makeicecream.com/makicecreami1.html
Discover how to make your own ice cream using two coffee cans

INDEX

ABOUT THE AUTHOR

Pam Rosenberg writes and edits nonfiction books for children. She lives with her family in Arlington Heights, Illinois. Ice cream is one of their favorite treats.

24